I0817474

THE *Booze-Free* BAR(C)ART BOOK

CECE BAILEY PAGE

4880 Lower Valley Road • Atglen, PA 19310

Books by the Author

THE BAR(C)ART BOOK:
The Art of Crafting Tasty and Timeless Cocktails
978-0-7643-6872-1

Library of Congress Control Number: 2025931631

Book cover, book design, and illustrations by Cece Page
Production design by Danielle D. Farmer
Editing by Kaylee Schofield
Author bio photography by Austin Martin
Introduction and outro photography by Calli Kennedy of The Living Lenz
Type set in Mrs Eaves OT/ Gotham

ISBN: 978-0-7643-7038-0
ePub: 978-1-5073-0620-8

Printed in China
10 9 8 7 6 5 4 3 2 1

Published by Schiffer Publishing, Ltd.
4880 Lower Valley Road
Atglen, PA 19310
Phone: (610) 593-1777; Fax: (610) 593-2002
Email: Info@schifferbooks.com
Web: www.schifferbooks.com

Other Schiffer Books on Related Subjects:
What's Your Potion? Liquid Refreshments to Nourish Body, Mind, and Spirit,
Morwyn, 978-0-7643-4954-6
Seasons Around the Table: Effortless Entertaining with Floral Tablescapes & Seasonal Recipes,
Jessie-Sierra Ross, 978-0-7643-6836-3

For my grandma.

Quilting, embroidery, gardening, baking, coloring, and mixing up sweet tea. . . All my first introductions to the creative process were because of her and I'm so thankful.

CONTENTS

Booze-Free BAR(C)ART

Welcome to season 2 of *The Bar(c)art Book* adventures! By the time you read this, I'll have a new baby in my arms, who unknowingly became the catalyst for this sequel.

If you read my first book, you know *The Bar(c)art Book* started as a passion project during the pandemic. I began mixing drinks, learning cocktail classics, and illustrating it all for fun. I eventually compiled it all into a recipe book. While the book's *content* was about crafting cocktails, the purpose was to illustrate that the *act of creating* is approachable and accessible to anyone. As with all creative outlets, I have found that the fun is in the process, and I wanted others to experience that too.

I received so much great feedback, but the biggest surprise was that readers appreciated the mocktail chapter more than anything else. Once I learned I was pregnant, I realized just how unaccommodating the world truly is to alcohol-free patrons. Almost everywhere I went, I was offered the same lame options of sodas or thoughtless mocktails that left me feeling both excluded and disappointed. It made me realize just how exclusive alcoholic beverages can be. And not the good kind of exclusive.

So many people don't consume alcohol for a variety of reasons, whether it's due to pregnancy, addiction recovery, mental wellness and clarity, or health restrictions—or maybe it simply isn't for their taste buds. So, why not make a sequel fully dedicated to the sober-curious souls out there? Zero alcohol and zero worries. Sounds like a winning recipe if you ask me.

This book contains 45 beautiful beverages that were crafted with you in mind. (And me! Hello, morning sickness.) Whether you're gearing up for a baby, hosting a thoughtful and inclusive gathering, or just want to sip on something with peace of mind, I hope you love what you find here.

Cheers friend,

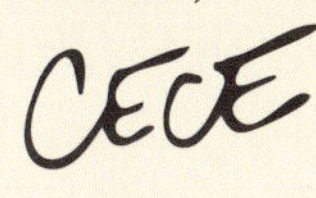

BAR TOOLS

Your bar needs only a few basic tools; the rest is fluff. Make sure you've always got the first two packed in your bag if you plan to play mixologist on a trip.

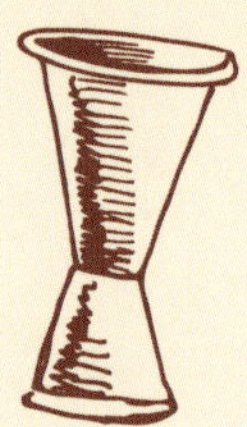

JIGGER

A jigger is your #1 most important tool. It's an hourglass-shaped measuring tool that is essential for making consistent drinks. The long end holds either 1.75 oz. or 2 oz. and is what you use for measuring out the base ingredient of your beverage. The short end is usually either 0.5 oz. or 1 oz. and is often used to measure things like simple syrup or secondary mixers.

SHAKER

There are many variations on a shaker, so play around with what kind you prefer. I have a few, but they all feature a built-in strainer that lets me pour my mixture straight into the glass after I've shaken.

BAR SPOON

A long, skinny spoon that is essential for stirring bevvies you build directly in the glass and stir to chill.

ICE MOLDS

Some drinks just require certain types of ice to be enjoyed properly. Invest in trays for large ice cubes, spheres, small ice cubes, and crushed ice to take your drinks to the next level.

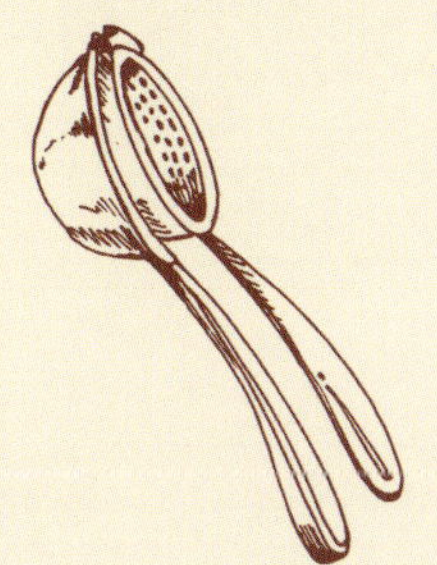

CITRUS JUICER

For me, this is essential. Almost anytime I mention a juice in this book, I'm implying that you squeeze that juice directly from the fruit. The best way to make a great libation is to use fresh ingredients whenever possible.

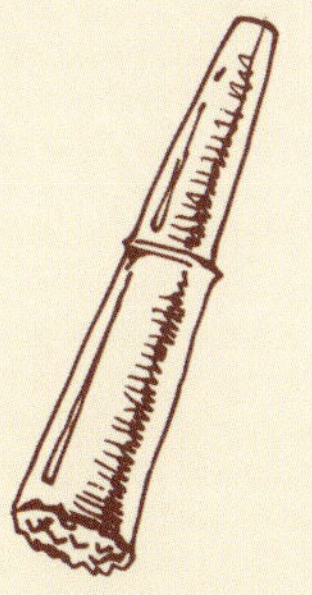

MUDDLER

This device is for crushing or mixing ingredients like mint or berries in your glass or shaker to express their essence.

SWIZZLE STICKS + SKEWERS

Presentation is a huge component of a good refreshment, and collecting beautiful skewers and swizzles to pair with your garnishes will make your drinks all the more memorable.

GLASSWARE

The variety in glassware is endless, but there are just a few variations you really need to make beautiful beverages. Certain glassware is also best suited for certain drinks and serves a real purpose, so it's important to know the goal of your drink before you pick its container.

You can find tons of great, affordable glassware online and in stores, but your local thrift shop is the best place to seek out hidden treasures. There are so many old, forgotten cocktail glasses at your neighborhood secondhand shop just waiting to be found. Your drink's vessel is just as important as the ingredients inside. I really encourage you to explore and find pieces that will be unique and make your bar special to you and your guests.

LOWBALL GLASS

Also referred to as the old-fashioned glass, whiskey glass, or rocks glass. This vessel usually has straight sides and a thick bottom to handle drinks that involve muddling. A glass that is known for drinks like the Old Fashioned and Negroni but is a universal shape that you can use for most drinks that include ice.

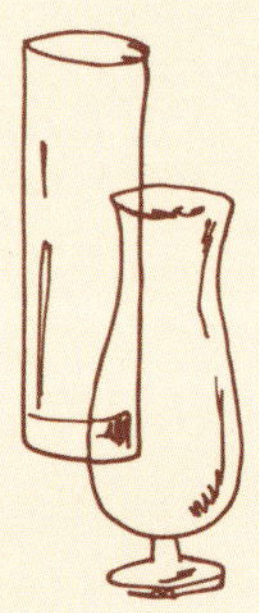

COLLINS GLASS

This shape is also referred to as a highball glass, and I tend to use the terms interchangeably. This tall, narrow shape is great for mixed drinks involving lots of ice or beverages that include components like ginger beer or club soda, since they minimize air exposure and keep your drink bubbly.

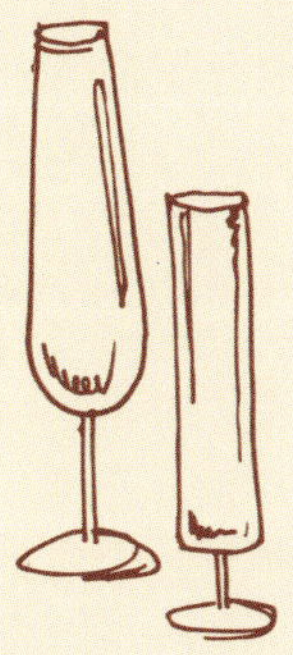

CHAMPAGNE FLUTE

This can sometimes be used interchangeably with a Collins glass and is ideal for any type of drink involving a bubbly component. Like the Collins, this glass shape protects carbonated drinks from losing their fizz but is a little more elegant if you're hosting an event with an air of formality to it.

MARTINI GLASS

Also referred to as the cocktail glass. This is the iconic, flared cup with a sleek stem that we all know, and can be used with any drink that is served chilled without ice.

COUPE GLASS

The coupe glass, sometimes called the saucer, is a wide, bowl-shaped glass that has made a resurgence in recent years. It began as a popular vessel for champagne but is bad at preserving bubbles and consequently has grown more popular with fragrant drinks that are served chilled.

Sweet + Smooth

I know you're supposed to save dessert for last, but this book is about bucking norms, so this chapter gets to go first. The ancient Egyptians, Aztecs, and Greeks all indulged in sweet treats like fruit, honey, and chocolate, so it seems it's always been human nature to partake in decadent things. Don't deny yourself, and have fun whipping up these candy-like concoctions.

LET'S MAKE THE:

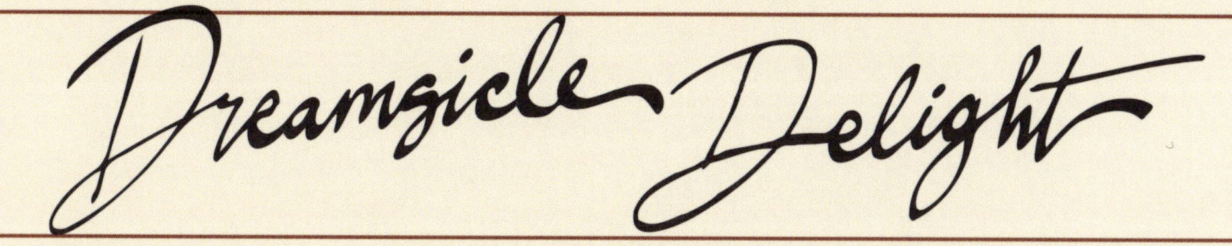

SERVES:

4

GLASS:

wine

INGREDIENTS:

12 oz. orange juice
4 tbsp. vanilla Greek yogurt
Orange Cream Poppi Soda
sliced strawberries or oranges

INSTRUCTIONS:

You will build this drink directly in each glass. Start by filling each glass with ice. Divide orange juice evenly among glasses and then add 1 scoop of Greek yogurt to each. With stirring spoon, combine each until mixture becomes a frothy pastel-tangerine color. Fill each glass to top with Orange Cream Poppi Soda. Garnish with your choice of a strawberry or orange slice.

NOTES:

I'm kicking things off with what might be my favorite recipe in the whole book; a drinkable version of a childhood staple, The Dreamsicle. Believe it or not, your favorite nostalgic treat was invented by an 11-year-old in 1905. Yes, you read that correctly. The first Dreamsicle, also known as the Creamsicle, was invented by an entrepreneurial child named Frank Epperson, who eventually grew up and sold the rights to the Popsicle company. Today, this iconic citrus-creamy flavor combo reminds us all to sit back and enjoy the simple things in life.

LET'S MAKE THE:

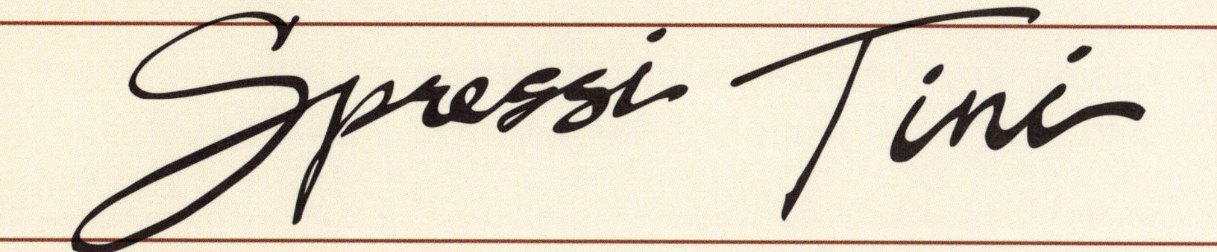

SERVES:

I

GLASS:

coupe or martini

INGREDIENTS:

2 oz. Three Spirit Nightcap
3 oz. Stumptown Cold Brew
0.5 oz. simple syrup
1 oz. coconut milk
0.5 oz. heavy cream (optional)
dash of cinnamon
coffee beans

INSTRUCTIONS:

Add all ingredients except coffee beans to a shaker with more ice than usual. Shake vigorously until frosty cold. Pour into your chilled glass and float a few beans on top for garnish. The heavy cream is optional for folks who like a sweeter martini.

NOTES:

There are two ways to create a nice foam on drinks you make. The first is to add an egg white to the recipe. The second is to add more ice than you usually use to the shaker and to shake for more time than feels natural. This allows more air to be introduced into the mix, creating bubbles that float to the top in a foam. Pouring your drink into the glass with a strainer on top also aids in the process, since it allows liquid to hit the glass first and pulls the foam back to the end of the pour.

LET'S MAKE THE:

Bailey Bramble

SERVES: 4

GLASS: lowball

INGREDIENTS:

muddled blackberries
2 oz. lime juice
2 oz. agave
1-2 12-oz. cans of blackberry seltzer
burnt/smoked rosemary for garnish

INSTRUCTIONS:

You will build this drink directly in each glass. Add 3-4 blackberries, 0.5 oz. agave, and 0.5 oz. lime juice to each glass. Muddle to release juices and turn fruit to a berry pulp. Add a large ice cube to each and fill to top with blackberry seltzer. Gently stir with your bar spoon. For garnish, lightly char strands of rosemary with a match and add to each drink.

NOTES:

Fun fact: I love this drink so much that Sawyer and I had it served at the cocktail hour of our wedding. I spent the day before muddling 2 large pots of blackberries by hand to give to the bartenders, who surely thought I was ridiculous and over-the-top. In doing this, I also dyed my cuticles purple 24 hours before my wedding—but it was definitely worth it for all our guests to have some tasty, berrylicious drinks!

LET'S MAKE THE:

Wascally Wabbit

SERVES:	GLASS:
1	coupe

INGREDIENTS:

2 oz. carrot juice
2 oz. pineapple juice
0.5 oz. lemon juice
nutmeg
cinnamon
1 egg white

INSTRUCTIONS:

Combine all ingredients in a shaker with ice and shake vigorously. Strain into a coupe glass and sprinkle a dusting of nutmeg on top for garnish.

NOTES:

I know Elmer Fudd hates to see this drink coming. But he should relax; there's no wabbits in sight. If you're hosting a Halloween gathering, consider floating a few pieces of candy corn on top to fit the theme. Since you'll have a lovely foam top (thanks to the egg white), you can throw any lightweight garnish you want on this wittle wascal.

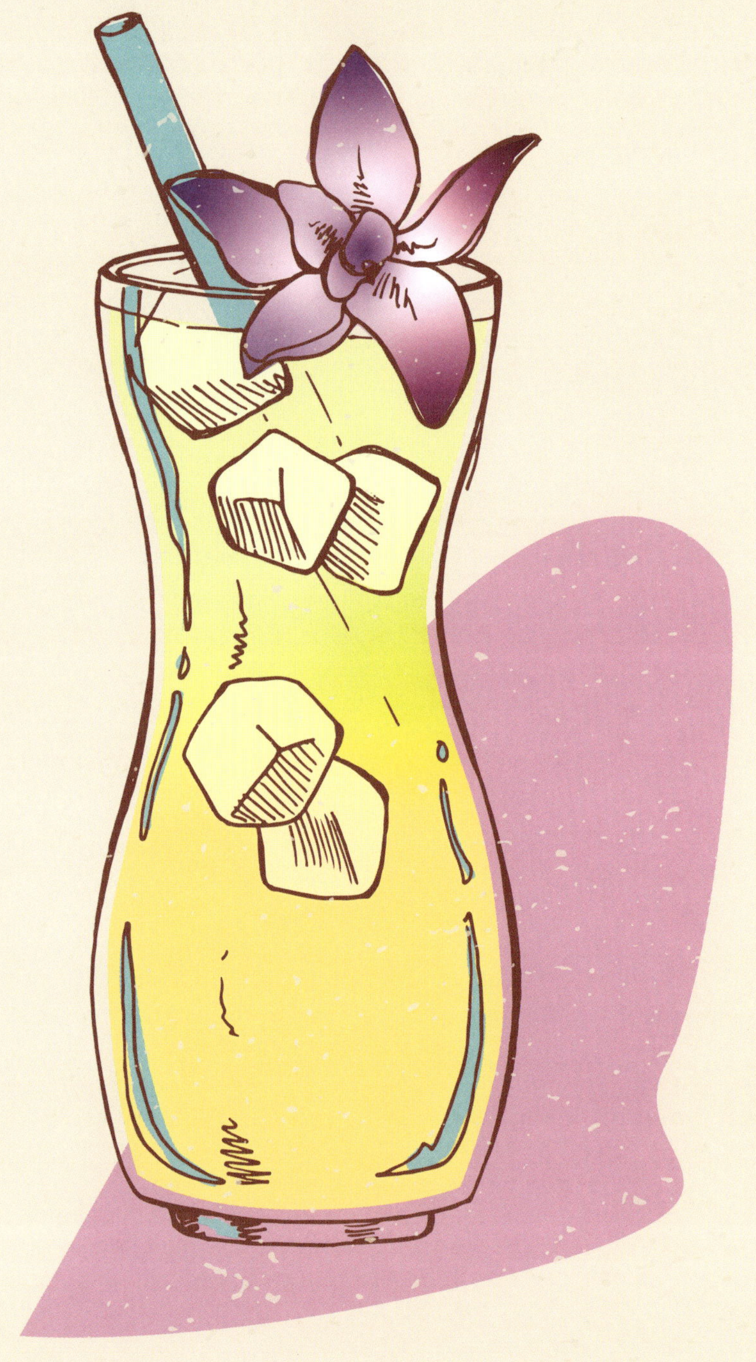

LET'S MAKE THE:

SERVES: 2

GLASS: Collins

INGREDIENTS:

4 oz. Lyre's White Cane Spirit
2 bananas
1 oz. lime juice
1 oz. simple syrup
8 oz. coconut milk
banana slices

INSTRUCTIONS:

Add all ingredients except banana slice garnishes to a blender with a large scoop of ice. Blend until smooth and pour evenly into two glasses. Garnish with your banana slices and a hibiscus flower if you're feeling tropical.

NOTES:

My husband and our friends took a bucket-list trip to Thailand in early 2024. It was truly the trip of a lifetime, with unforgettable views. We snorkeled with sharks, visited elephants at a sanctuary, and, most importantly, drank banana daiquiris with a monkey at a beach bar. Both the monkey and the daiquiri were the highlight of my trip, so this drink is dedicated to that wonderful bevvie.

LET'S MAKE THE:

Red Cherry Disco Ball

SERVES: 4

GLASS: Collins

INGREDIENTS:

2 oz. maraschino cherry syrup
4 oz. cold brew
Mexican Coca-Cola
heavy whipping cream
maraschino cherries (optional)

INSTRUCTIONS:

Fill your glasses with ice and drizzle 0.5 oz. of maraschino cherry syrup in each. Add 1 oz. of cold brew to each drink and then fill nearly to the top with an ice-cold Mexican Coke. Add a splash of heavy whipping cream on top and garnish with a few maraschino cherries if desired.

NOTES:

Drinks like this one are all about the presentation. Consider leaving the glass untouched once you add the cream, so that those gorgeous swirls can take center stage for a moment as the cream and cola mix. Adding a colorful straw as a swizzle stick allows your patron to stir the drink up into a frothy sweet treat when they're ready.

LET'S MAKE THE:

SERVES: I

GLASS: coupe

INGREDIENTS:

3 oz. pear juice
0.5 oz. lime juice
1 egg white
cinnamon
2 dashes Angostura bitters
fresh figs

INSTRUCTIONS:

Combine all ingredients except figs in shaker with ice and shake vigorously. Strain into a coupe glass. Cut a fig in half and thread on a cocktail skewer. Gently place on top of drink for your garnish.

NOTES:

This bevvie comes out in a beautiful pale pink hue—just like my birthstone, which it's named for. Shoutout to all the well-balanced Libras out there. We are a superior astrology sign and don't let anyone tell you otherwise.

LET'S MAKE THE:

Lonesome Dove

SERVES:

4

GLASS:

lowball

INGREDIENTS:

cinnamon sugar rim
8 oz. apple cider
2 oz. lime juice
4 oz. pineapple juice
Olipop Crisp Apple
nutmeg and cinnamon
cinnamon sticks

INSTRUCTIONS:

Using a lime slice, rim your glasses and then dip in a cinnamon-sugar mixture. Fill glasses halfway with ice. In your shaker, combine apple cider, lime juice, pineapple juice, nutmeg, and cinnamon with ice. Shake vigorously and then distribute between glasses. Top each off with Olipop and garnish with cinnamon sticks.

NOTES:

Only one thing to do when the leaves start to change ... mix this drink up and exclaim, "It's fall, y'all!" to no one in particular. If you want to add an extra kick to your libation, grab a pack of spicy ginger beer at the store and up the ante.

LET'S MAKE THE:

Sorbet Float

SERVES: 4

GLASS: martini

INGREDIENTS:

muddled raspberries
2 oz. lime juice
8 oz. pineapple kombucha
4 scoops of raspberry sorbet
mint leaves

INSTRUCTIONS:

Muddle raspberries and lime juice in a mixing glass until raspberries are a fruity pulp. In each martini glass, add a large scoop of raspberry sorbet. Gently distribute the raspberry mixture between your four glasses and then top each off with pineapple kombucha. Take care to pour liquids around each scoop to avoid premature melting. Slap fresh mint leaves against the back of your hand to release their scent, and put one on top of each sorbet scoop to garnish.

NOTES:

In the absence of ice during this bartending process, consider sticking your glasses in the freezer for an hour or so before making these so that your glass (and the sweet treat inside) are served frosty cold. You can swap the sorbet and kombucha flavors for whatever your heart desires, so get creative!

Bubbly + BRIGHT

The first "spritz" originated in Italy, as do most good things in life. During the 1800s, various Austrian soldiers, merchants, and other travelers who wandered through the Veneto region of Italy found the wine being served too strong for their taste. It became customary for patrons to request a *spritzen* or "spray" of water in their sparkling wine in order to dilute it. That means the first spritz drinks were actually a very early shift toward today's ever-growing trend of lower-ABV and mocktail beverages. Today, there are so many options for a carbonated component to build bubbly drinks you'll love, and we have the trendsetting Europeans to thank for that. Now that's *amore*.

Topo Chico
Topo Chico
MINERAL WATER

LET'S MAKE THE:

Ladybird

SERVES:

1

GLASS:

Collins or Topo Chico bottle

INGREDIENTS:

Topo Chico
2 oz. pineapple juice
2-3 dashes Angostura bitters
lime wedge

INSTRUCTIONS:

In a Collins glass filled halfway with ice, add 2 oz. pineapple juice and 2–3 dashes of bitters before filling to top with Topo Chico. Garnish with a lime wedge. Alternatively, open a cold Topo Chico and pour out 1–2 oz. Replace with pineapple juice and bitters before adding a playful straw for garnish.

NOTES:

This is my go-to order at bars and restaurants that are lacking in the mocktail department. You can request this in a highball glass or have them build it directly in the Topo Chico bottle. I personally love the latter with a fun straw.

LET'S MAKE THE:

SERVES:

4

GLASS:

Collins

INGREDIENTS:

sliced cucumbers
8 oz. Seedlip Garden 108
2 oz. lime juice
4 oz. lavender syrup
tonic water
lavender or rosemary sprigs

INSTRUCTIONS:

Peel a cucumber lengthwise so that you have 4 thin strips. Wrap each one around the wall of your glass before filling with ice. In each glass, pour 2 oz. Seedlip, 1 oz. of lavender syrup, and 0.5 oz. of fresh lime juice. Fill each to top with tonic water before gently stirring with your bar spoon. Garnish with lavender sprigs or lime wheels.

NOTES:

Folks tend to think flavored simple syrups are tough to create, but the process couldn't be easier. Simply combine 1 part water and 1 part sugar in a pot on the stove and bring to a boil. Once bubbling, lower heat to a simmer and add your flavored element (in this case, fresh lavender sprigs). Cover and keep heat on low for 10–15 minutes, stirring occasionally. Allow to cool, strain sprigs, and pour into a mason jar. Keep it in your fridge for up to a week!

LET'S MAKE THE:

Botanica

SERVES: 4

GLASS: lowball

INGREDIENTS:

2 oz. lemon juice
Raspberry Rose Poppi
club soda
edible flowers or
lemon twist

INSTRUCTIONS:

Fill your glasses halfway with ice. Add 0.5 oz. lemon juice to each. Fill halfway with Poppi and then fill remainder of space with club soda. Stir gently with your bar spoon. Garnish with edible flowers or a lemon twist.

NOTES:

This drink is perfect for a garden party soirée. You can find edible flowers at specialty grocery stores or head out to your backyard and snip a few fresh from the stem. Pansies, hibiscus, marigolds, lavender, and chamomile are all great garnish options.

LET'S MAKE THE:

Peachy Keen

SERVES: 6

GLASS: lowball

INGREDIENTS:

2–3 peaches, chopped
3 oz. lime juice
3 oz. simple syrup
mint leaves
ginger beer
peach slices

INSTRUCTIONS:

In each glass, drop a scoop of gooey peach goodness. Add 0.5 oz. lime juice, 0.5 oz. simple syrup, and a few mint leaves to each before muddling well until pulp is blended. Fill all to top with ginger beer and stir with your bar spoon. Top each off with a fresh peach slice.

NOTES:

Save this one for summertime, when the farmers' markets are in full swing. Fresh peaches from a local farm really do taste that much better. If you have the time and want to maximize the flavor for a large batch of drinks, throw your sliced peaches in a pan on the stove with sugar and simmer on low for 10–15 minutes for a delicious gooey purée.

LET'S MAKE THE:

Dolly Parton

SERVES: 4

GLASS: flute

INGREDIENTS:

2 oz. lemon juice
1 oz. simple syrup
Fre Brut Sparkling non-alcoholic wine
lemon peels

INSTRUCTIONS:

In each flute glass, pour 0.5 oz. lemon juice and 0.25 oz. simple syrup and fill to top with sparkling NA wine. Express a lemon twist above each and drape on rim for garnish.

NOTES:

Dolly is one of my all-time favorite musicians and philanthropists. She is fabulous, generous, and always sparkly. And of course, a lemon peel on top is a nod to her platinum blonde locks. If you're feeling extra Dollylicious, add a sprinkle of edible glitter to each glass for some extra glam.

LET'S MAKE THE:

Troublemaker

SERVES:

4

GLASS:

wine

INGREDIENTS:

1 can of pear halves
2 oz. lime juice
Fre Brut Sparkling non-alcoholic wine
lime peels (optional)

INSTRUCTIONS:

Open your can of pear halves and remove solid pieces of pear, leaving juice behind. Distribute roughly 1 oz. of pear juice into each glass and then add 0.5 oz. of lime juice to each. Fill to top with sparkling NA wine. Garnish with a lime twist if desired.

NOTES:

I know I always harp on about squeezing fruit juices fresh for your drinks, but I often break my own rules. This is a great example. The sickeningly sweet syrup that pears are canned in is actually the perfect ingredient to balance out some brut bubbles.

LET'S MAKE THE:

Kiwi Crush

SERVES: 4

GLASS: lowball or Collins

INGREDIENTS:

3-4 kiwis, sliced
4 oz. lime juice
2 oz. simple syrup
mint leaves
lime slices
club soda

INSTRUCTIONS:

In each glass, add kiwi slices, mint leaves, 1 oz. lime juice, and 0.5 oz. of simple syrup. Muddle until juices are well-expressed. Add ice halfway in each. Fill to top with club soda and stir gently with your bar spoon. Garnish with additional mint leaves and kiwi slices.

NOTES:

A good mojito can utilize any fruit, but the mint is always going to be the superstar. Believe it or not, your nose experiences mint leaves much more than your taste buds do. Because of this, your garnish is especially important here. Mint is most fragrant when it's shocked in ice water and slapped on the back of your hand just before serving. Your patrons will find themselves sniffing this drink as much as they sip it.

LET'S MAKE THE:

C'est Si Bon

SERVES:

4

GLASS:

flute

INGREDIENTS:

4 oz. strawberry syrup
2 oz. lime juice
Prima Pavé NA Rosé Brut
strawberries for garnish

INSTRUCTIONS:

Make strawberry simple syrup ahead of time and allow to cool. When it's time to serve, add 1 oz. of strawberry syrup and 0.5 oz. of lime juice to each flute. Top with NA rosé. Slice additional strawberries and add to rim of glass for garnish.

NOTES:

Some of the earliest varieties of strawberries originated in French forests. France is also the top producer and consumer of rosé. As someone who conducted quite a bit of field research during my trips there, I can verify that both products are of top quality. So this is a sweet, spritzy ode to the good things in France ... and life!

LET'S MAKE THE:

Hugo Spritz

SERVES: 4

GLASS: wine

INGREDIENTS:

4 oz. elderflower syrup
lemon bitters
Prima Pavé NA Blanc de Blancs
club soda
lemon wheel
mint leaves

INSTRUCTIONS:

Fill your glasses halfway with ice. In each, add 1 oz. of elderflower syrup and a few dashes of bitters. Fill each halfway with NA sparkling wine. Fill to the top with club soda and garnish with fresh mint leaves and lemon wheels.

NOTES:

Unlike its well-known bitter cousin the Aperol Spritz, the Hugo is light and refreshing with notes of lemon and florals. It was originally crafted in northern Italy near the Austrian border by bartender Roland Gruber, who used fresh elderflowers. Thankfully, today, elderflower syrup is readily available at your local grocery store, and it's a great ingredient to keep in stock in your fridge. Anytime you want to add a floral essence to your beverage, a splash of this syrup will do the trick.

Tart + TANGY

Tart and tangy drinks stand in a class of their own. In fact, the term "sours" refers to an entire category of cocktails in the beverage world. The stars of these drinks are always the flavors of citrus or acids. Cherries, grapefruits, limes, lemons, blood oranges, tomatoes, and more come together to form an unlikely team that packs a real punch. Any good tangy drink contains a base liquid, a sour-flavored superstar, and a touch of sweetener to keep things balanced. However, everyone has a different level of tolerance with sour elements, so you have the power to tweak the ratios on the following pages to suit your taste buds.

LET'S MAKE THE:

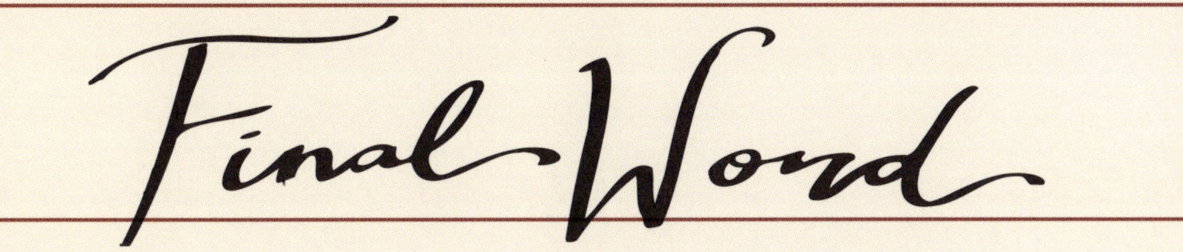

SERVES: 1

GLASS: coupe

INGREDIENTS:

0.75 oz. Free Spirits The Spirit of Gin
0.75 oz. Ghia NA Apéritif
0.75 oz. tart cherry juice
1 oz. lime juice
brandied cherry

INSTRUCTIONS:

Combine all liquid ingredients in your shaker with ice and shake until cold. Strain into your coupe glass and garnish with a skewered brandied cherry.

NOTES:

Consider this the little sister of the ever-popular Last Word cocktail. I absolutely love sour and tangy flavor profiles, so I knew this was one cocktail I would have to reimagine to tickle my tastebuds just right. You can also garnish with your favorite piece of sour candy to really wow the crowd.

LET'S MAKE THE:

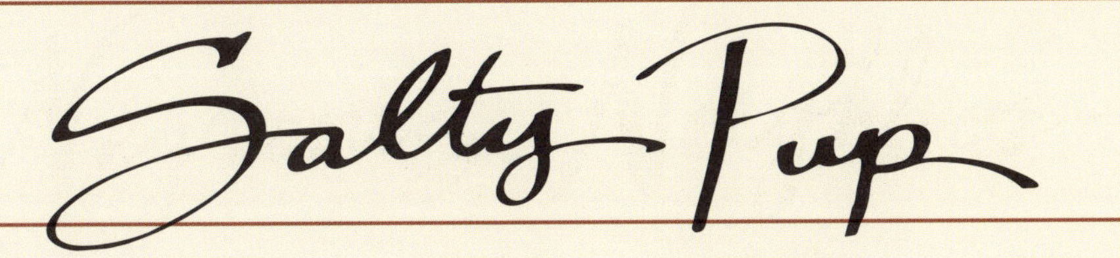

SERVES:

2

GLASS:

Collins

INGREDIENTS:

salt
2 oz. grapefruit juice
2 oz. blood orange juice
2 oz. simple syrup
grapefruit soda
citrus slices

INSTRUCTIONS:

Rim both glasses by running your grapefruit along the edges and then dipping in salt. Fill each glass halfway with ice. Combine all liquid ingredients except your soda into a shaker with ice and shake vigorously. Strain evenly into your two glasses and fill to top with soda. Stir gently before garnishing with citrus slices of your choice.

NOTES:

The first Salty Dog drink dates back to the 1920s. Like all good beverages, the recipe is simple, but the key is using fresh ingredients. This is one recipe where I really encourage you to squeeze some fresh citrus juice for optimal flavor.

LET'S MAKE THE:

Hail Mary

SERVES: 2

GLASS: Collins

INGREDIENTS:

12 oz. tomato juice
2 oz. olive brine
2 oz. lemon juice
hot sauce
Worcestershire sauce
cayenne pepper
black pepper
celery
pickle
olives
lemon wedges

INSTRUCTIONS:

Fill glasses halfway with ice. To each, add 1 oz. olive brine, 1 oz. lemon juice, splash of hot sauce, splash of Worcestershire sauce, cayenne, and black pepper. Fill remainder of glasses with tomato juice and gently stir with your bar spoon. Garnish with remaining ingredients for final touch!

NOTES:

This book is about drinks, obviously, but a good Bloody Mary also counts as a snack. The garnish game is everything here, and there are no rules. You can add bacon, pickles, olives, cheese cubes, a chicken tender, and anything else you can think of! Don't forget your rim either; bagel seasoning, chili powder, salt, and Tajín are just a few options for adding an extra element to the mix.

LET'S MAKE THE:

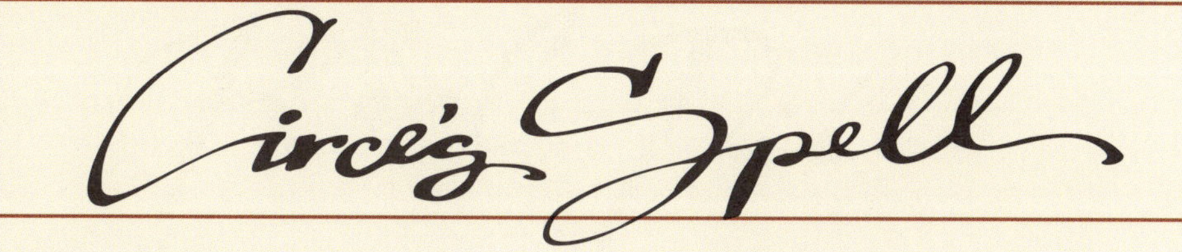

SERVES:	**GLASS:**
2	lowball

INGREDIENTS:

Tajín
1 celery stalk
1 jalapeño pepper
1/4 cup cilantro
4 oz. lime juice
2 oz. agave
club soda
lime slices
jalapeño slices (optional)

INSTRUCTIONS:

Rim your glasses with Tajín and fill each halfway with ice. In a blender, combine all remaining ingredients except for your lime wheels, jalapeño slices, and club soda. Blend until smooth and then distribute mixture evenly among your glasses via a strainer to remove any solid pulp. Fill each to top with club soda and gently stir with your bar spoon to combine. Float a lime wheel and a few jalapeño slices on top for garnish.

NOTES:

In Greek mythology, Circe is the daughter of the sun god Helios and the ocean nymph Perse. She lives on a secluded island and becomes notorious for crafting potions from herbs and plants in her garden, albeit sometimes for sinister reasons. This drink is a toast to that mischievous, green-thumbed goddess.

LET'S MAKE THE:

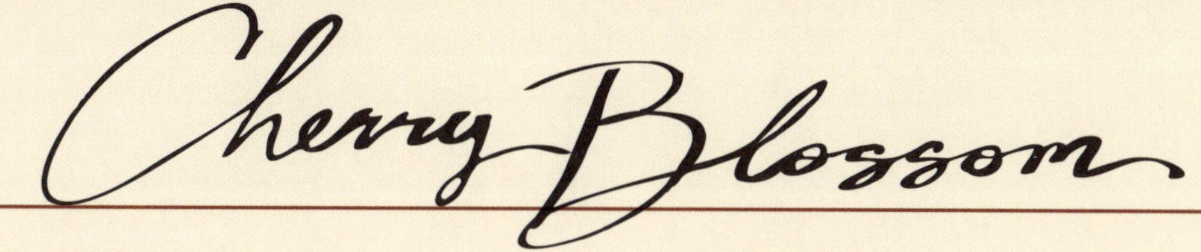

SERVES: 2

GLASS: Collins

INGREDIENTS:

1 oz. Lyre's Apéritif Rosso
1 oz. lime juice
2 oz. cherry juice
1 oz. agave
Cherry Limeade Poppi
maraschino cherries

INSTRUCTIONS:

Fill your glasses halfway with ice. In a shaker combine Lyre's, lime juice, cherry juice, and agave with ice. Shake vigorously. Strain into your glasses and top with Cherry Limeade Poppi. Garnish with a few maraschino cherries.

NOTES:

If you save this recipe for your next springtime soirée, you can snip a few actual cherry blossoms from the tree as they bloom, to use as garnishes. In the Southeast, that typically occurs in the last weeks of March or early April.

LET'S MAKE THE:

SERVES:

4

GLASS:

lowball

INGREDIENTS:

Tajín
8 oz. passion fruit juice
2 oz. lime juice
2 oz. agave
4 oz. pineapple juice
passion fruit, halved

INSTRUCTIONS:

Rim your glasses with Tajín and fill each halfway with ice. Add all liquid ingredients to a shaker with ice and shake vigorously until cold. Strain into your glasses. Next, scoop the pulp from each passion fruit half into each drink and stir together. Garnish the drinks with an additional passion fruit half on a cocktail skewer.

NOTES:

Passion fruit is a severely underappreciated fruit here in the USA. Keep an eye out for it at the grocery store in the summer, and if all else fails, settle for the juice or purée sold on shelves. If you get your hands on the actual fruit, don't be scared of the seeds. They have just as much flavor as the pulp and add a fun crunch to drinks.

LET'S MAKE THE:

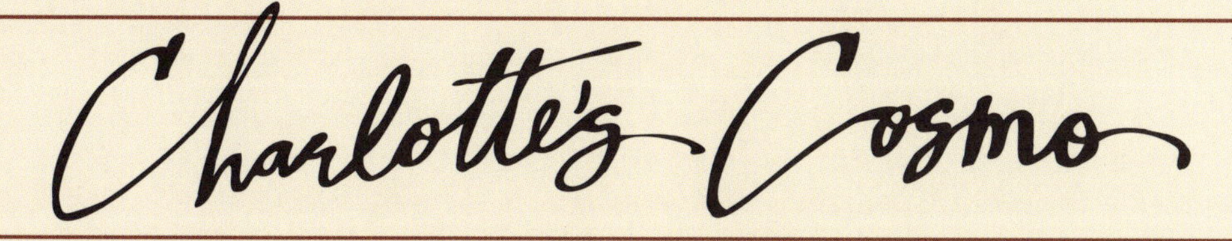

SERVES: I

GLASS: martini

INGREDIENTS:

2 oz. Ritual NA Vodka
2 oz. cranberry juice
1 oz. lime juice
1 oz. orange juice
lime wheel

INSTRUCTIONS:

Combine all ingredients except lime wheel in shaker with ice. Shake vigorously and then strain into martini glass. Garnish with lime wheel or lime twist.

NOTES:

Cosmos never go out of style, and they're fun to enjoy year-round. If you're making this during the holidays, add a sugar rim and garnish with cranberries. For Valentine's, skewer strawberries instead. If it's summertime and 80° out, go for a lemon twist.

LET'S MAKE THE:

Ghia Spritz

SERVES: 4

GLASS: Collins

INGREDIENTS:

4 oz. Ghia NA Apéritif
tonic water
lemon twists

INSTRUCTIONS:

Fill your glasses halfway with ice. In each, pour 1 oz. of Ghia NA Apéritif. Fill to top with tonic water and express a lemon twist on the top before dropping in for garnish.

NOTES:

Tonic water and club soda truly are interchangeable, but it's important to sample both and figure out which flavor you prefer. Tonic water has a distinctly citrus note that hits the front of your mouth, which is why I paired it here with Ghia. Club soda feels more neutral in flavor and is great for simply adding carbonation to your drink. Know you can always swap them to utilize the one you like best.

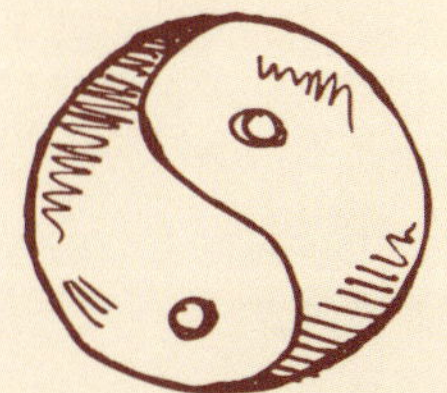

Savory SURPRISES

This chapter is named Savory Surprises because the next few recipes might strike you as weird, but just trust me and give them a try. Sometimes ingredients that seem like polar opposites can combine to create something strangely magical. Sort of like Martha Stewart and Snoop Dogg's friendship. It never made sense before we saw it with our own eyes, and now we can't get enough.

LET'S MAKE THE:

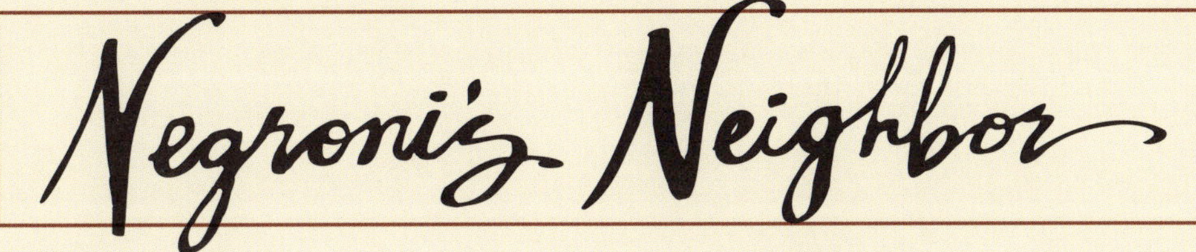

SERVES:

I

GLASS:

lowball

INGREDIENTS:

I oz. Lyre's Apéritif Rosso
I oz. Ghia NA Apéritif
0.75 oz. Free Spirits NA Gin
orange or lemon bitters
orange peel

INSTRUCTIONS:

You'll build this drink directly in your glass. Start by placing a large rock ice cube in and then adding all other liquid ingredients. You will need only 2–3 dashes of bitters. Slice off an orange peel and run it along the rim of the glass. Twist to express it over your drink before dropping it in as garnish.

NOTES:

The original Negroni was born from Count Camillo Negroni ordering a variation of his regular drink, the Americano, in a bar in Florence, Italy. Throughout history and to this day, it's still a common drink that patrons order variations of; different base liquors, added splashes of champagne, or chocolate bitters instead of orange are just a few of the common requests. It only makes sense that this booze-free version serves as yet another iteration of this classic. If you aren't crazy about the bitterness, add a splash of citrus juice and NA sparkling wine to make it more to your liking.

LET'S MAKE THE:

Coconut Telegraph

SERVES: 2

GLASS: lowball

INGREDIENTS:

Tajín
4 oz. Lyre's White Cane Spirit
4 oz. cream of coconut
2 oz. lime juice
1 oz. simple syrup
chopped jalapeño
additional jalapeño slices

INSTRUCTIONS:

Drizzle lime juice on the side of your glass and dip in Tajín. In your shaker, combine all liquid ingredients and a few jalapeño slices. Shake vigorously until cold and then strain into your glasses. Float a few jalapeño slices on top for a spicy garnish.

NOTES:

Drinking this tropical conconction is like taking a mini adventure. There's a kick of heat at the end, but the creamy coconut and acidic lime balance everything out nicely. This is a great recipe to make at the beach or your next backyard barbecue. Sip sip hooray!

LET'S MAKE THE:

Real Dill

SERVES: I

GLASS: martini or coupe

INGREDIENTS:

2 oz Seedlip Garden 108
1.5 oz. pickle juice
1 oz. olive brine
celery bitters
olive oil
gherkin pickle garnish

INSTRUCTIONS:

Combine Seedlip, pickle juice, olive brine, and bitters in a shaker with ice. Shake vigorously until cold. Strain into your glass. Drizzle a few olive oil drops on top for presentation. Add a skewered gherkin pickle on top for additional garnish.

NOTES:

I expect this recipe to receive raised eyebrows and mixed reviews. But that's okay, it's not for everyone. However, if this drink is right in your lane and you want to give it a little extra kick, swap the olive brine for pepperoncini juice!

LET'S MAKE THE:

SERVES:

4

GLASS:

lowball

INGREDIENTS:

4-5 banana slices or 1 oz. creme de banana syrup
2 tsp. brown sugar
2 tsp. maple syrup
8 oz. Three Spirit Nightcap
cinnamon (optional)

INSTRUCTIONS:

In each lowball glass, add a few banana slices, 0.5 tsp. brown sugar, 0.5 tsp. maple syrup, dash of cinnamon, and a splash of warm water. Muddle until it's well-blended and banana chunks are smooth. Add a large rock ice cube and then pour 2 oz. of Three Spirit in each. Stir gently with your bar spoon to cool drinks down. Garnish with a dusting of cinnamon on top. Substitute banana slices with a banana syrup if you prefer a smoother drink without pulp.

NOTES:

Similar to banana bread, this drink works best with those overripe bananas that are starting to go brown on your countertop. The mushier they are, the sweeter they'll make this drink (and they'll be easier to muddle). Definitely all monkey business here.

LET'S MAKE THE:

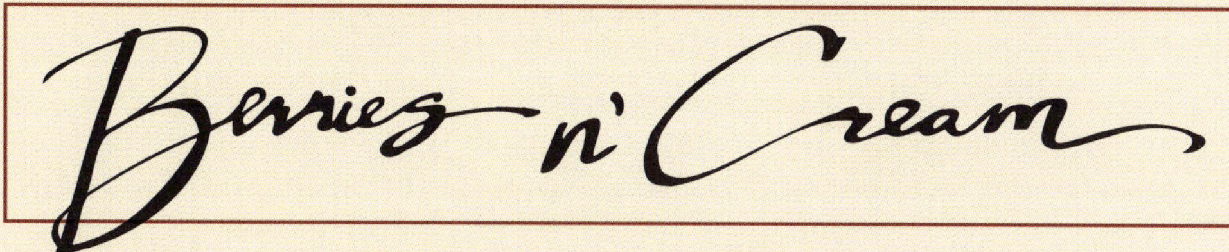

SERVES:

2

GLASS:

lowball

INGREDIENTS:

4–5 strawberries
4 oz. aloe vera
4 oz. coconut milk
4 oz. pineapple juice
2 tbsp. maple syrup
shredded coconut

INSTRUCTIONS:

Combine everything except shredded coconut in a blender and blend until smooth. Place a large rock ice cube in each glass and strain in mixture. Garnish your drinks with a sprinkle of shredded coconut on top.

NOTES:

While aloe is well known as an antioxidant-packed sunburn treatment, it's wildy underappreciated as a drink ingredient. Consuming aloe aids in digestion, can regulate blood sugar, has been shown to relieve gum and oral pain, and is an excellent source of hydration for your skin. Drink up!

LET'S MAKE THE:

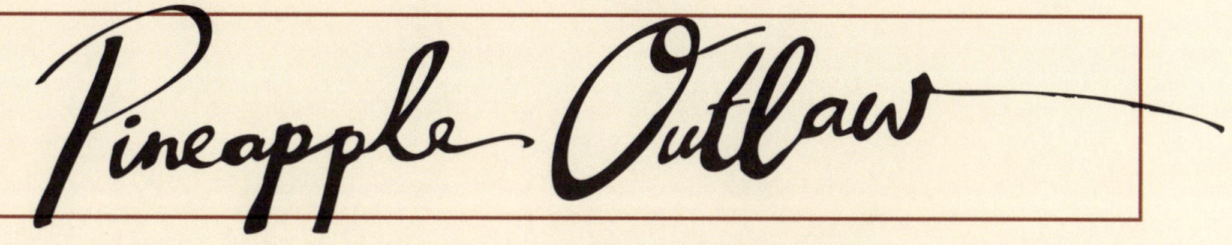

SERVES: 2

GLASS: lowball or Collins

INGREDIENTS:

Tajín
ginger root, chopped and mashed
1/2 chopped jalapeño
2 oz. agave
2 oz. lime juice
Angostura bitters
4 oz. pineapple juice
ginger beer

INSTRUCTIONS:

Rim your glasses with Tajín and then fill each halfway with ice. In your shaker, add chopped jalapeño, ginger root, agave, lime, and lime juice. Muddle well until ginger and jalapeño are crushed into a rough pulp. Add your pineapple juice and ice. Shake vigorously until cold. Strain evenly into your glasses. Fill remainder of glasses with ginger beer and stir with bar spoon to combine. Garnish with a few extra jalapeño slices on top.

NOTES:

Pineapples are originally from South America. They were distributed and traded to Europe and America beginning in the 1600s. Because of the exorbitant cost of importing, pineapples became a symbol of wealth and were often displayed as centerpieces at dinner parties, remaining untouched and uneaten until they rotted. A classic and tragic case of keeping up with the Joneses. Thankfully, today, we all know and appreciate how delicious fresh pineapple juice is.

LET'S MAKE THE:

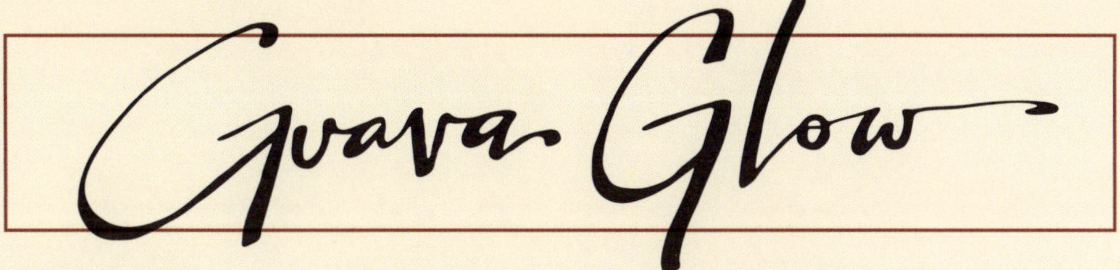

SERVES:

2

GLASS:

lowball

INGREDIENTS:

sugar or salt for rim (optional)
4 oz. guava nectar or purée
2 oz. coconut milk
1 oz. lime juice
6 oz. Lime LaCroix

INSTRUCTIONS:

Run a lime slice on the rim of your glasses and then dip in sugar (or salt if preferred). Combine all ingredients except for sparkling lime water into a shaker with ice and shake vigorously until well chilled. Distribute evenly between two lowball glasses filled with ice. Fill to rim with sparkling water. Garnish with a lime slice or tropical flower for added flair. Add a few extra jalapeño slices on top.

NOTES:

The ingredients of this one really are the three musketeers, and you can tweak proportions to get the flavor profile you like best: sweet, tangy, or bubbly. A fun way to dress this drink up is to try out flavored salts. Pink Himalayan salt and lavender hibiscus salt are two options I keep in my pantry, and they also add an unexpected pop of color.

LET'S MAKE THE:

Ice Spice

SERVES:

2

GLASS:

coupe or wine

INGREDIENTS:

sugar for rim
3 oz. spiced syrup
4 oz. cranberry juice
1 oz. lime juice
Sprite
cranberries for garnish (optional)

INSTRUCTIONS:

Rim your glasses with sugar. If using wine glasses, add ice to halfway in each. In your shaker, combine spice syrup, cranberry juice, and lime juice with ice. Shake until ice-cold. Strain evenly into glasses. Top off each with Sprite. Garnish with a few cranberries if desired.

NOTES:

To make the syrup for this drink, combine 1/2 cup of maple syrup with 1–2 chipotle peppers, 1 tsp. of cayenne pepper, 1 tsp. cinnamon, 1 tsp. of red pepper flakes, and a splash of water in a blender to combine. This will produce enough for roughly 4–8 servings depending on how spiced you'd like your drinks to be.

LET'S MAKE THE:

Green Mermaid

SERVES:

1-2

GLASS:

Collins

INGREDIENTS:

4 stalks celery, ends trimmed
1 large leaf of kale, stem removed
2 honeycrisp apples, cored
1 cucumber
2 oz. lime juice

INSTRUCTIONS:

You'll need a juicer for this one, but trust me, it's worth it. Juice all ingredients via electric juicer. Squeeze your limes via a handheld juicer and add to mix. Stir well and pour into an ice-filled Collins glass.

NOTES:

This is a fabulous drink to start your day off with. Fresh fruit juices are hard to beat. If you're making these as bevvies to serve for a gathering, consider switching to lowball glasses filled with ice, filling each halfway with this mixture, and topping with a bubbly herbal element like a cucumber seltzer.

LET'S MAKE THE:

Hot Toddy

SERVES:

4

GLASS:

thermal mugs

INGREDIENTS:

- chopped and peeled ginger root
- 3 lemons, juiced
- 4 tsp. cayenne pepper
- 2 oz. maple syrup
- cinnamon sticks
- 8 cloves
- 2 black tea bags

INSTRUCTIONS:

Combine all ingredients except tea bags in a pot with 4–6 cups of water and bring to a boil. After mixture reaches boil, drop to a simmer for 5–10 minutes. Add tea bags in for the last 5 minutes to allow them to steep. When ready to serve, remove tea bags and any large solid pieces, like ginger root and cinnamon sticks. Carefully ladle your hot drink into each mug and garnish with a floating clove or cinnamon stick. Serve immediately.

NOTES:

You can use any tea for this recipe. I like black tea, but a few nice caffeine-free options include chamomile, peppermint, and ginger teas. If you're feeling under the weather, this is also a great drink to clear your sinuses and keep you cozy!

LET'S MAKE THE:

SERVES:

4-8

GLASS:

lowball

INGREDIENTS:

1 can cream of coconut
8 oz. coconut milk
4 oz. Beckett's '27 NA
Cinnamon Whiskey
4 tsp. vanilla extract
8 oz. chai tea, cooled
cinnamon
nutmeg
black pepper
cinnamon sticks
whipped cream
(optional)

INSTRUCTIONS:

Combine all ingredients except cinnamon sticks and whipped cream into a blender with a handful of ice. Blend until smooth and then chill in the fridge for 12–24 hours before serving time. Once ready, pour into lowball or Collins glasses, top with whipped cream, and garnish with cinnamon stick.

NOTES:

It seems like islanders just have good taste. Take this drink, for example. While traditional eggnog is delicious, this Puerto Rican version is simply a step above. Colloquially known as the coquito, creamy coconut and chai flavors create the coziest drink, perfect for holiday hosting.

Party PICKS

Although all the recipes in this book can be multiplied if you're hosting a party, this chapter is specifically filled with drinks you can easily make in batches with minimal tools, medium effort, and maximum impact. I love to host parties, and the growing frequency of baby showers happening in my life means about half of attendees are usually pregnant or under the age of 10. Therefore, it only makes sense to have a parting party chapter to close out this book!

LET'S MAKE THE:

SERVES:

10-12

GLASS:

lowball

INGREDIENTS:

1 bottle sparkling white grape juice
2 oz. lemon juice
honeydew + cantaloupe blended, strained
mint leaves
frozen melon balls

INSTRUCTIONS:

Chop a large, ripe melon and put in blender. Strain into a pitcher and add lemon juice, mint leaves, and sparkling grape juice. Put in fridge to chill until ready to serve. In each glass, drop a frozen melon ball, fill with melon mix, and garnish with fresh mint leaves.

NOTES:

Grab an additional melon before you prep for this recipe. Chop in half and use an ice cream scoop to carve out spherical melon balls. Stick in a bowl in the freezer 24 hours before your gathering. When it's time to serve, use these in place of ice cubes.

LET'S MAKE THE:

Summer Lovin'

SERVES:

10-12

GLASS:

lowball

INGREDIENTS:

1 medium watermelon
10 oz. lime juice
5 oz. basil simple syrup
Watermelon LaCroix
basil leaves
Himalayan salt or
 Maldon coarse salt
 (optional)

INSTRUCTIONS:

Make your basil simple syrup the day before and keep chilled in fridge. An hour or so before gathering, chop up your watermelon and combine it in the blender with lime juice and simple syrup. Blend until smooth and strain into a pitcher to remove any solid bits. Chill in fridge. When ready to serve, fill glasses halfway with ice. Pour your mixture into each glass until halfway full. Top each off with watermelon LaCroix and garnish with basil leaves.

NOTES:

Remember being a kid in the summer? Nothing was better than running around all day, jumping in and out of a body of water, and being handed a slice of watermelon with a sprinkle of salt on top. There's a reason that flavor combination is tried and true. If you want to give your guests a little taste of nostalgia, add salt rims to your drink with something like Himalayan pink sea salt or Maldon coarse salt.

LET'S MAKE THE:

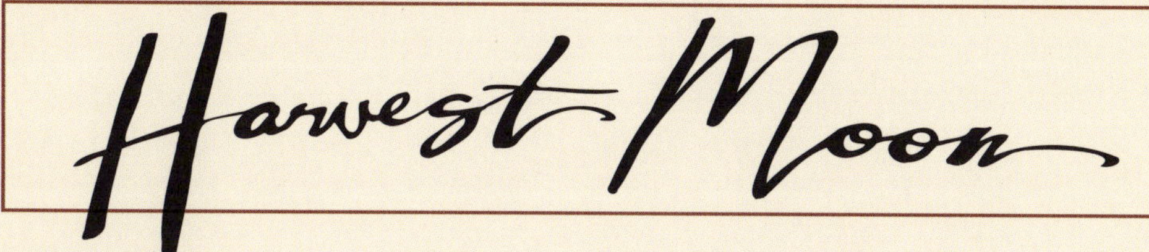

SERVES:	**GLASS:**
10-12	lowball

INGREDIENTS:

16 oz. cranberry juice
16 oz. orange juice
16 oz. ginger beer
16 oz. Sprite
cinnamon
cloves
nutmeg
rosemary
cranberries

INSTRUCTIONS:

Prepare this an hour or so before your gathering. Add equal parts cranberry juice, orange juice, ginger beer, and Sprite to a large pitcher. Every pitcher is sized differently, so adjust your recipe accordingly. Add a few dashes of cinnamon and nutmeg along with a handful of cloves before stirring to combine. Chill in the fridge until ready to pour. Fill your glasses halfway with ice before pouring in drink. Garnish with sprigs of rosemary and sugary cranberries.

NOTES:

This one is for your next holiday party, when those big bags of fresh cranberries start showing up in the grocery store. In a bowl, coat said cranberries in lime juice before dipping in a secondary bowl filled with sugar. Put them on a plate in the freezer until ready to serve. At party time, float them as a garnish as you mix drinks for a festive, snow-dusted aesthetic.

LET'S MAKE THE:

SERVES: 10-12

GLASS: lowball

INGREDIENTS:

1 gallon blue Hawaiian punch
16 oz. pineapple juice
1 liter Sprite
2–3 scoops vanilla ice cream (optional)

INSTRUCTIONS:

Combine all ingredients in a large punch bowl. Consider floating playful elements like rubber duckies on top to fit the occasion. If you're hosting a kiddo's birthday party, setting out glasses with balls of cotton candy in each is also a fun way to let guests interact with the drink-making process as they pour their own glasses.

NOTES:

It's pretty easy to mix up pink or peachy-toned punches, but it's a lot harder to make a blue one. In honor of my baby boy on the way, here's a fun aqua punch you can use next time you host a shower or birthday party.

LET'S MAKE THE:

SERVES:

12-16

GLASS:

lowball or Collins

INGREDIENTS:

2 black tea bags
6–7 lemons
1-2 cups of granulated sugar
water
mint leaves

INSTRUCTIONS:

In Pot #1 on the stove, bring 2 cups of water to a boil. Turn off heat, add 2 tea bags, and let steep for 10–15 minutes. Add 2 cups of cool water and then pour into party pitcher. In Pot #2, bring 1–2 cups of sugar and 1 cup of water to a boil until sugar dissolves. Let cool and add to pitcher. Juice approximately 6 lemons and add lemon juice to pitcher. Fill pitcher the rest of the way with cold water, about 2 cups. Add mint leaves to pitcher as the mix cools, and store in fridge. Pour over ice and garnish with lemon wheels.

NOTES:

Sweetheart, welcome to the sugary South. One of my favorite memories from childhood is making sweet tea with my mom and grandma in the kitchen. I would dutifully stand on a chair and watch as the tea was boiled, steeped, and transferred to the pitcher. I was then tasked with the important job of adding sugar. I recall using a large soup ladle to drop unbelievable amounts of sugar into the steaming mixture and watching it instantly dissolve in swirls. These days, I love the classic Arnold Palmer mix with a (slightly) less sweet tea and fresh-squeezed lemons for a beautifully balanced drink.

LET'S MAKE THE:

SERVES:

10-12

GLASS:

lowball or wine

INGREDIENTS:

8 oz. orange juice
4 oz. lime juice
chopped apples
chopped strawberries
orange slices
raspberries
1 bottle of NA red wine
6 oz. Sprite
6 oz. ginger ale

INSTRUCTIONS:

Place chopped fruits, orange juice, and lime juice in a pitcher. Use a spoon or muddler to express fruit essence and create a mashed blend. Add your bottle of NA wine. Stir to combine and add Sprite and ginger ale to your liking. Put in the fridge to chill overnight before serving in lowball glasses filled with ice.

NOTES:

Sóller is a relatively isolated mountain town that we visited on the island of Mallorca in Spain. It's obviously a tourist hotspot but is also well-known among Spaniards for its plentiful citrus groves. You can only imagine how delicious the sangria is there. Sangria is commonly thought of as an alcoholic beverage, but in Spain, it's enjoyed by folks of all ages and is often crafted in a booze-free form for events such as children's birthday parties.

LET'S MAKE THE:

SERVES:

10-12

GLASS:

lowball

INGREDIENTS:

12 peaches, chopped
1 cup sugar
4 oz. lemon juice
4 oz. lime juice
club soda
mint leaves
lime slices

INSTRUCTIONS:

Combine peaches, sugar, and citrus juices in a blender. Blend until smooth. In a pitcher, add desired amount of mint leaves and muddle to express flavor. Pour in peach blend and fill to top with club soda. Toss in additional peach slices for presentation. In glasses, fill halfway with ice before pouring drink in. Garnish with lime slices.

NOTES:

You can prep the peach blend portion of this recipe ahead of time, but wait to add your club soda until it's party time. As with all carbonated elements, timing is everything. You don't want your drink to fall flat, so wait until just before serving to add your club soda to the mix.

LET'S MAKE THE:

SERVES:

10-12

GLASS:

lowball or beer mugs

INGREDIENTS:

2 liters cream soda
4 tbsp. butterscotch syrup
1 cup heavy whipping cream
2 tbsp. powdered sugar

INSTRUCTIONS:

In a large pitcher, combine cream soda and butterscotch syrup. Stir just enough to combine flavors, and set aside in fridge to chill. In a mixing bowl, beat heavy cream with a stand mixer or whisk until peaks form. Add sugar and continue to whisk until mixture becomes fluffy. Distribute your chilled drink into each glass and add a large dollop of whipped cream on top. Drizzle additional butterscotch syrup on top as a final garnish.

NOTES:

After visiting the Wizarding World of Harry Potter, I knew I would have to create a Butterbeer dupe at home. Much to my husband's shock (and disgust), I guzzled about five separate servings of this delicious concoction in between rollercoaster rides during our visit. I simply couldn't get enough. This is a great drink for your next Harry Potter movie marathon day or Halloween party. Not only is it super sippable, but it's ridiculously easy to whip up for a big crowd.

SUBSTITUTIONS

If you don't have the exact ingredients listed in the recipes, that's fine! Here are some suggested substitutions.

SUGGESTED INGREDIENT:	SUBSTITUTES:
Beckett's '27 NA Cinnamon Whiskey	Spiritless Kentucky 74 Spiced NA Cinnamon Whiskey Lyre's Amaretti Caleño NA Rum Dark & Spicy
Fre Brut Sparkling Non-Alcoholic Wine	Mionetto Sparkling NA Wine Surely NA Sparkling Brut Giesen NA Sparkling Brut Lyre's Classico NA Sparkling Wine
Free Spirits The Spirit of Gin	Lyre's Dry London Spirit Ritual Zero Proof Gin Alternative CleanCo Clean G Gin Alternative
Ghia NA Apéritif	Lyre's NA Italian Spritz San Pellegrino Sanbittèr Red Lyre's Italian Orange
LaCroix Lime	Lime Topo Chico Spindrift Lime Liquid Death Severed Lime
LaCroix Watermelon	Waterloo Watermelon Sparkling Water Watermelon Poppi Soda Liquid Death Convicted Melon Sparkling Water
Lyre's Apéritif Rosso	St. Agrestis Phony Negroni Blutul NA Rosso Vermouth Little Saints NA Negroni Spritz Sparkling Cocktail
Lyre's White Cane Spirit	Ritual Zero Proof Rum Alternative Caleño Light & Zesty Tropical NA Spirit Beckett's '27 NA Coconut Rum
Olipop Crisp Apple	IZZE Sparkling Apple AVEC Fuji Apple & Cardamom Betty Buzz Sparkling Apple Ginger Sour Cherry Mocktail

Pineapple kombucha	Pineapple juice Health-Ade Tropical Pineapple Kombucha GT's Golden Pineapple Kombucha Wildwonder Pineapple Paradise Sparkling Prebiotic
Poppi Cherry Limeade	IZZE Sparkling Cherry Lime IBC Cherry Limeade Favorite Day Cheery Cherry Lime Soda
Poppi Orange Cream	Jones Orange & Cream Soda Stewart's Orange n' Cream Soda OLIPOP Orange Squeeze
Poppi Rose Raspberry	Fentimans Botanically Brewed Rose Lemonade Belvoir Farm Elderflower & Rose Lemonade Something & Nothing Hibiscus & Rose Premium Soda
Prima Pavé NA Blanc de Blancs	Giesen NA Sauvignon Blanc Surely NA Blanc Le Petit Étoilé NA Chardonnay
Prima Pavé NA Rosé Brut	Mingle NA Sparkling Raspberry Rosé Noughty NA Still Rosé Wine Giesen NA Rosé
Ritual NA Vodka	Monday Zero Alcohol Gin Roots Divino NA Aperitif Bianco Seedlip Garden 108 Free AF NA Vodka Spritz
Seedlip Garden 108	Lyre's Pink London Spirit Lyre's Dry London Spirit
Three Spirit Nightcap	Free Spirits The Spirit of Bourbon Spiritless Kentucky NA 74 Bourbon Lyre's Traditional Reserve Lyre's Coffee Originale NA Spirits
Topo Chico	Maison Perrier Ultimate Sparkling Water Mountain Valley Sparkling Water Liquid Death Sparkling Mountain Water

FINAL THOUGHTS

I always like to say I'm an enthusiastic amateur in everything I do, which means I don't consider myself an expert in anything. These recipes showcase what I find tasty, but we're all different—so take these as a starting point and edit amounts and ratios as you see fit. YOU are the expert on what is best for you. Next time you find yourself in a setting that isn't quite inclusive enough, remember that you have the agency to craft a drink and environment that suits your taste.

Cheers!

(C)ECE PAGE

Cece Page is the author and illustrator of *The Bar(c)art Book* and *The Booze-Free Bar(c)art Book*. She lives in Atlanta, Georgia, with her husband, son, and two pups.

Cece is a full-time graphic designer and artist who enjoys bringing creative ideas to life for her clients.

You can reach out to her directly at:

the-cece-shop.com

DRINK LIST